FINISHING LINE PRESS

www.finishinglinepress.com

Waiting for Someone to Find Me

poems by

Francine E. Walls

Finishing Line Press
Georgetown, Kentucky

Waiting for Someone to Find Me

For Chris

ACKNOWLEDGMENTS

Arnazella: "Sauk River, North Fork"
Avocet: "Prism"
By & By: "Elegy"
damselfly review: "On the Welsh Coast"
Ekphrasis Journal: "Rendezvous"
Forage Poetry: "Prodigal"
PoetsWest: "Fragility"
Pontoon: An Anthology of Washington State Poets: "Taneum Creek"
Scarlet Leaf Review: "An Affair of Dreams;" A Sibling Visits the Cloistered
Convent (for Karen)"
Writing Across Cultures: A Handbook on Writing Poetry and Lyrical Prose:
"Kalahari Desert"

Publisher: Leah Maines
Editor: Christen Kincaid
Cover Art: Francine E. Walls
Author Photo: Jayne Marek
Cover Design: Elizabeth Maines McCleavy

Printed in the USA on acid-free paper.
Order online: www.finishinglinepress.com
            also available on amazon.com

Author inquiries and mail orders:
Finishing Line Press
P. O. Box 1626
Georgetown, Kentucky 40324
U. S. A.

Table of Contents

Prodigal

That moment you know you are lost,
each rolling ridge of yucca, a duplicate,
the bandit sun steals your water, salt.
The desert locks shut against you,

sets thorns, cat claws, spines—
needle-sharp. You are lost
in foothills amid stiff winds.
You grab cacti, hear ravens

as you stumble, fall on a rosette of bayonets.
The boulders beside you once billowed
obsidian plumes of rock. Cooled, eroded.
Wind and rain carry dust to the sea.

Do not be afraid. This fire cooks our changes.

At dusk, the gnarled pinyon pine
blackened in death is a silhouette
against the loosening sun.
Ankle swollen, your slab of body

drains among the cholla
under the moon's bright eye.
Yet, even now you are sought,
the prodigal returning home.

With flares alight, the helicopter
churns up each arroyo seeking sign.
Do not hide.
Sing like the owl in the juniper.

Sweet Water

Every living thing on earth
needs water,
even that tiny patch of black
on desert sand
that formed its world
as a kind of sponge,
that holds the water
that came so briefly—
like love, perhaps,
felt once and held as memory,
as sustenance
against all odds.

Taneum Creek

I tent in an ancient flood plain.
Yellow-jackets end their frenzied quest
for food among the chili cans and leave the camp at dusk.

As light dims above me, grass on the hill turns golden,
columns of basalt blend together into one,
a glimpse into a fluid past before the lava cooled.

I reach for the lantern, blister my thumb.

The crickets barely sing above the creek's roar.
Full moon glows low on the horizon
through the lodge pole pines.

If only childhood were a room
I could walk away from,
soften the voices, close the door.

At the water's edge, I slip my hand
under the glacial stream and let the throb
of the burn from the lantern fade.

What Could Go Wrong in the Desert?

You are lost.
Your phone. Useless.

A thunderstorm washes out the road.
You drive down a steep hill and cannot get back up.

The car gets stuck in the sand.
Rocks puncture the gas tank,

all the gas leaks out.
Flash floods bury the car.

Rain soaks your cotton shirt and shorts.
The wind picks up.

Hiking, you fall off a boulder and knock yourself out.
Revived, you slip onto sharp rocks cutting your femoral artery.

The day gets hotter.
You have no hat, no long sleeves.

A scorpion, snake or brown recluse spider bites you.
You have an allergic reaction.

A swarm of bees surrounds you.
You run out of water.

In the desert, the wrong road can kill you.

Geologist, Anza-Borrego Desert

Left in the ignition, the key
is worn down almost straight now.
On the dash, a pack of Camels
rests on maps among rock samples

and tufts of green tamarisk.
Shirtless, he leans forward, turns the key.
A birthmark flutters over his sixth vertebrae,
a length of key-chain disappears

near a triangle torn on his khaki shorts.
He pushes his hair back from his forehead,
presses the gas petal,
takes a hard right. The key falls to the floor,

yet he roars on at dawn, oblivious.
A hand lens sways on a cord around his neck.
Among trackless valleys,
purple mountains in the distance,

he lurches past one arroyo
on the way to the next
seeking sign of what
will shatter the earth.

Hacienda del Sol

Timing may be almost everything.
First, put water on to boil,
instant coffee only, though we have cream.
Cut up strawberries bought
from a fruit stand on the road to the desert.

Find a skillet in the tiny kitchen,
ant trap in the corner.
No scorpions on the deck
because they sprayed for them this morning.
Brown a little butter, crack in eggs.

Set out jam, salt and pepper.
The doves coo-coo outside the door.
A prickly-pear cactus blooms deep yellow.
Flash of purple, a hummingbird's iridescence.
Ocotillo shoots its long red petals

from the green of its thorny sleeves.
Already the deep blue of sky quibbles
with the heat. Eggs done—not too hard,
not too runny, the way he likes them—
slip onto a plate, butter muffins, pour coffee.

Assemble everything on a tray. Carry it to the patio,
set before the geologist staring
at the Santa Rosa Mountains,
gazing four million years into the past, then,
a million years into the future.

He cracks open fossils of hummingbirds, homo sapiens, scorpions.

Fork.
Spoon.
Knife.

Here. Eat while it's hot.

The Pleiades

Pearl, oyster, agate—desert hues—fade.
Camped in the creased arroyo,
I lie on the hood of the truck.
Stars emerge horizon to horizon,

the Pleiades a glow of light above Orion's belt,
a meteor flashing out in death,
a satellite tumbling from its orbit, winking out a life.
When you can't go on with someone, what then?

He left his cooler, tent, butane stove in the camp,
left this place gouged out by floods
where cacti jump toward movement,
granite traps quartz crystals.

Only the crackle of the fire
until the shriek of a hunting hawk.

By the apricot moon,
tiny desert trumpets bloom
where saber-tooth tigers once pounced on prey,
moths flutter straight into the fire.

Beatitudes

A fish jumps in the placid cove startling the water
rushing away in concentric rings.

An orca pod threatens a mother seal and baby,
black knife in blue water, black heads bobbing, disappearing.

A flimsy raft off Tripoli—migrants—
a mother face down in a sinking boat,

her baby drifting away, limbs moved only by water,
limp, unknowing sea creature.

Off Italy, off Greece, hear murmurs of the rescued
moans of the drowning.

Here, the thug of a great blue heron
scouts the entire cove for food, announcing himself harshly.

The moon rose last night, higher and higher,
rosy glow filling the undulating distance.

Listen as the mourning doves sing
antiphonally
across the cove to each other.

The tide will rise twice today, fall twice.
Sometimes this is all the breath the earth will share.

Cottonwoods

Circlets of fluff in the corner,
some gather below the window
opened wide, a halo
of jasmine on the bed-stand,

the tea in the cup still warm,
slight bitterness of flowers long-steeped.
I touch the triangles of your body,
trace the space between your thumb and forefinger,

the crook of your elbow, split of your legs,
the curve of scapula.
You smile as hummingbirds chirp among the feeders,
ruby feathers glowing like blood,

as if plumeria could bloom in the garden
and oranges ripen this far north.
You roll me in your arms.
Your blue veins send messages to mine

of *plenty   plenty   plenty*

Through the Looking Glass

Your hands
rough and thick,
loosen the fragrance of timber
under the blade of your saw.
You mount one stone upon another,
walling off the orchard from the deer.
You sow patterns of wheat, soy, rye
that quiet our hunger.

If we lie close together
under the cherry tree
whose blossomed-boughs almost touch earth,
and if we braid our long hair together
into one long braid,
you, with your gentle hands
now thin, soft and deft,
could easily tuck in this strand of memory.

Band Leader

Piano,
your fingers run scales
   up and down my spine.
A shadow of a Nina Simone
   sings ocean-deep, comes breathing hope,
   comes curving and curling.

Alto sax,
tie me up tight,
      drink my gin,
      loosen my goose.
Fly me to the lost
then rescue me
with a skin-tight kiss and your thigh-high jasmine.

Horns,
vibrate in the marrow of your arms and legs
   around me,
   blow fast and hard,
   your blue eyes
   blur,
   belly to belly.

Call out to your savior, I'll call out to mine.
   Take your solo with me.
   Take my wallet.
   Take every regret.

Pianissimo,
   pluck every string in our blue rendezvous,
      a quiet tinkering with fire.

Fragility

The mother's breathing is
classroom-perfect. Sun
then moon set upon her labor
as she pushes, pauses,

gasps. Hours ago, the midwife
left the birth to doctor, nurse,
a hard birth, like a task
set by a difficult

teacher. Feet
clasped in the stirrups, baby caught
tight beneath her flesh.
Metal fingers grip

fragile cheekbones,
mixing blood of mother, child.
The clock on the wall
opens wide each minute,

still not enough space
for tiny shoulders
to make the passage until
within a moan   the snap

of a clavicle, and then
the ominous murmur of the infant heart.

Kalahari Desert

The principal's wife
hides her prosthetic arm
so life-like under her sleeve.
She walks me to the tenant farmers
and their cisterns on the hill.

Dry season is here,
as maize becomes dust
even thorn-scrub withers.

Our pump has lost the will
to suck water from the dry-river sand.

Cockroaches crowd
beneath Degas' portrait
of Mademoiselle Malo
hung high in my rondavel
close to the thatched roof.

Grasses hum.
I skirt the dark places
scorpions, black mambas hide.

Flying termites wallow in dirt,
burrow to coolness and mate,
abandoning wings
to lay eggs.

Mealie meal, butter beans
and goat meat: rank, tough, salty.
Nothing to drink.

The tenant farmers' sheds defy habitation.
Evicted families coalesce on the steps,
their need for water
fallen from maize
to cattle, to children.

We step closer to the water.
When farmers in Setswana plead
with the principal's wife,
her good arm
waves them away.

As children watch,
we dip our bottles
in the cistern
reflecting the cloudless sky.

Sauk River, North Fork

Sauk River, North Fork,
flows strong at Sloan Creek,
bends past red-headed birds
hopping from alder to alder
free of canopy.

Like the birds, do you come here often,
pondering a billion galaxies,
the speed of light,
slow eons since creation,
responsible deaths and radiant lies?

Are you jerked from season to season unwillingly,
clinging like a shy child to mother's leg,
longing for mottos to live by,
miracle cures,
guarantees, insurance?

You abandon trails
undermined by rotting bridges
above sheer cliffs
below rock falls.

At the summer trailhead,
tent pitched near ancient trees
their corrugated bark soft with moss,
you grieve fallen red cedars
whose long bodies nurse tiny hemlocks.

Hoof prints in morning mud
appear near cinquefoil,
golden on green,
bleeding heart, skunk cabbage,
elderberry, dwarf dogwood.

After Decades of Schooling

After decades of schooling, a friend
poses this question
over the telephone:

Was King George VI
the man
his father was?

Did I know once?
Methinks
what I have read

left mostly sediment,
dim recollections, residues
like the hot springs

at Yellowstone
where elk
lie on broad terraces,

as mineral water
drips down
to lower levels,

or evaporates
leaving gold and orange,
so, on cloudless

August days
a herd of elk
can lie

in warm and shallow water
on a bed of soft sediment
among good friends.

Emergency Poem

This is the poem for emergencies,
like the spare batteries and extra gas
you pack when you drive into the wilderness.

When you discover you are lost,
you can press any word in this poem,
and walk beside calm waters.

This poem does not have
water, food, shelter or energy bars,
yet courage is hidden in every line.

Before you crumple up this poem,
feeling danger north, south, west, east,
remember love's gift to you: your next breath.

An Affair of Dreams

I have etched him into my garden
among the nocturnal lilies,
again and again amid the brief, white lilies.
He has gone into soil, to humus,
my hands caress its darkness.

I mold this soil around the roots of plants
stolen from a green house,
their tiny roots untested by rain or wind.
They may take hold and grow into bristlecone pines,
or a forest of birch,

or an avalanche of poppies.
This soil will never diminish
but erupt replenished, ripe with life.
Only then, will I let him feed me blueberries,
tiny tomatoes, sweet as candy.

A Sibling Visits the Cloistered Convent
for Karen

Sister Mary of Christ leans toward me,
our forefingers touch, then hook around each other
through iron lace dividing the cloistered room,
the air in the convent still as the cross.

In her black habit, she talks of boysenberries
tied up carefully on horizontal wires, carrots thinned
to the call of songbirds and her ceaseless
prayers for the outside world.

Finishing my news of parent and brother,
I feel my slow-burning anger,
her semi-annual letters that arrive promptly
like the bell that calls her away to vespers.

Prism

Come back, dearest heart!
The garden suffers with me in winter.
The crows screech in the firs.
Raccoons sleep in the fennel
tamping down the leaves
smelling of licorice.

Silently, crocuses will
raise their silken heads,
clumps of purple.
Then, the yellow ones will rise,
thin leaves arch.
Too soon they will fade into soil.

The birdbath stutters in wind and rain,
waves lap and overlap.
See the way the bright water
casts off the past,
casts off its glittering colors,
casts off the shape of your face.

Rendezvous

Down to the nameless pond, the geese
honking at stragglers,
gliding to rest among the reeds,
goslings trailing in open water.

A Steller's jay cries its hoarse cry.
The pond in August now low, the foliage
thick enough to hamper my trail to the boulder
lying close to the water's edge,

the great rock laden with huckleberries
whose roots clutch thin lichen.
The maples already in their changes
drop their yellow messages.

Bats emerge at dusk,
careen across the pond,
sketch jagged streaks in the darkening sky
writing of all things lucid.

On the wall in my room,
over the coverlet of rosebuds
a painting glows in the dark—
the four-masted schooner anchored offshore

while on the sand a skiff lies at an angle,
gathered around by men in bright sweaters.
I imagine the squawk of herons, the scent of salt.
The ocean pushes up a river,

the river pushes back, then pauses,
until the tide recedes pulling the river with it
and eons convene as droplets of mist
on this near eternal shore.

Serpentinite Rock

You, my beloved, a volcanic core,
a monolith of andesite,
rise from sea waves,
resisting each swell of wind, water,
eroding will, eroding time.

Ocean waves cannot best
or break you, my stalwart sentinel,
my guard. Your detractors
thrash among the kelp and sea grass.

You, the uplifted seabed, merge
into new land—
cut, grazed, pierced, plowed.

The giant, long-horned bulls
mellowing in sun scatter at your step,
lavender star-flowers billow at your feet.
Cow herds run with joy,
black silhouettes on green tufts of tapestry.

Your flanks soft as young
horses near reedy ponds
filled with frog-songs and redwing
blackbirds as church bells ring.

You, the jagged peak of serpentinite rock,
the skin of earth slips to reveal you.
Lichen-rich boulders lurch into meadows
echo the clash of sea floor and tectonic plates.

Let me yellow up the pastures
with mustard blooms, orange the cliffs
with poppies. Let your hands quickly
grow your wine, sweet and tart,
near the wrinkled sea.

Crack me open,
set to vigil, set to ripeness.
Enjoy me forever.

Petroglyph, Furnace Flats, Grand Canyon

Woman of the Old Ones,
a stranger stood in your home today
amid the rubble of the slate walls,
cool to the touch in the heat,
and watched the Colorado River in the canyon far below.

Old Woman,
your pots lie shattered in the red soil
among the mounds of Brittlebush that dot the talus slope.
The open bowl, the special one, glazed orange,
drawn with geometric forms,
rests broken below the ragged precipice.
Every ceremony finished,
every act complete.

Old Woman,
the grinding stone of your metate
fits smoothly in the palm of a hand.
On the shards of water jugs,
the mark of your thumbnail etching clay remains,
    soft a thousand years ago.

To your daughters and the wives of sons,
each word you gave sang rhythms of the earth:
    Leave and return
    Expand and contract
    Lead and follow.

You taught them
    what erodes and what does not,
    how to dye the colors of the Canyon into thread
        and weave them amber, cinnamon and gold,
            emerald, pink.

Every sorrow now forgotten, every fear erased:
  the failing of the summer rain and winter snows,
  the boulder rolling down, inexorably,
    knocking your husband from the trail,
  and your child, dipping water from the river,
    pulled beneath the rapids.

Old Woman,
the canyon wrens flee up the gully.
No watchmen stand in the high places.
The granaries are empty,
the mortar smashed.
No corn, no beans, no squash.

Still, circles chiseled on the rock,
petroglyphs, guard the steep path down to the river.
Raccoon leave their tracks at the creek at dawn.
Side-canyons bloom with golden columbine,
                    red-bud and cardinal flower.
The herons stalk in the shallows then rise with steady wings.
The moon glows full on the red-rock walls
and a scent like jasmine fills the air.

Tell the raven that glides across the highest cliffs,
tell the rain in dark clouds,
tell the strangers,
Woman of the Old Ones,
tell them you are never far from home.

Love Story and War

You have been careless of me,
leaving me in the meadow,
the pasture of winter elk.

In the field, you push snow with your shovel in bursts
down to the brown soil
urging its fruitfulness with your sweat.

I look up at you from the freezing earth,
look into your blue eyes,
your arms, powerful from working the farm.

The pumpkins you gathered from spent vines
lie piled up, then boiled, then ladled into jars and set in the cellar,
enough pumpkin soup to staunch your hunger for a year or more

Stop.

You have been careless of me in dreams.
Once again, you *walk point* in war, fourteen days in a row,
at every turn, the first in the sniper's fire. Every step into the haze, you
thought

Stop.

You come to me in my dreams,
kissing my forehead
in the weary years, the shrapnel-through-the-bone years,

through the war that might have killed you,
though the world has turned uncounted times
since you said, *No more.*

Go.

Sanctuary

When I am turned to ash,
I want you knowing
that I hear your footfalls
in the ancient forest,
the scream of hawks,
the water crazy-mad flowing
down to the sea,

and I want
you knowing
that I see you
on your knees in the garden,
your hands among the colors
of poppies, begonias, columbine and larkspur
that grow beneath you, beside you,

and I want you
knowing that I feel
your beating heart,
a still-questing spirit,
so, when I am ash,
even with all that has happened,
you will have these words.

Learning to Walk Again

Perhaps, this is like learning to walk again,
gripping the parallel bars,
dragging my feet along,
sending impulses from my brain,
pull in, *ad*duction—pull out, *ab*duction
bend in, bend out,
over and over again,
and still my feet cannot hold my weight.

Perhaps, this is like learning to use my wrists again,
rubbing the white spots of scars
where the nails held my bones in place,
now trying to pinch a button
between thumb and forefinger,
pick it up and put it in a box,
over and over again,
and still I cannot lift a thimble's weight.

Perhaps, this is like learning to speak again,
moving the reluctant tongue
to the precise place needed,
sounding out the vowels and consonants
over and over again,
as if this language were foreign
to the shape of my mouth,
and still I cannot bear a greeting's weight.

Perhaps, this is like learning to hear again,
after word reached me of his death,
that ceaseless tinnitus
clicking, hissing, roaring, ringing,
over and over again,
as if the nerve cells of the cochlea
strive to drown out every other sound,
and still I listen only for his voice,
that lovely and familiar weight.

Loneliness

One clove of garlic, chopped,
sautéed in olive oil,
a handful of spinach leaves
steamed, rice noodles boiled.

    An Arctic freeze
    settles on the city
    too dry for snow,
    the ground frozen and stiff.

    A squirrel walks the top
    of the fence toward the firs
    looking for something tasty,
    finding nothing.

Place setting for one
at the table, a vase of roses
flown in from Chile this morning,
dark now at every window.

The Coming Eclipse

The sea carves out the land.
The stream running
down to the head of the cove
pulls down the soil of its banks,
pressing the roots of fir into salt water.

Each curve of the beach
is edged in such brightness,
light strong enough
to walk upon, a path
anyone with desire could take.

> *On the beach,*
> *seagulls battle for a dead shark,*
> *(eyes gone, spine exposed,*
> *tail gnawed),*
> *until my dog chases them away.*

> *On the land,*
> *I plant a red-bud maple,*
> *I throw a stick for my dog*
> *who retrieves it but will not give it up,*
> *shaking the stick back and forth.*

I will swim to the bottom of the cove,
lie down in the field of sand dollars
slanted, imbedded,
seaweed in my hair,
salt in my mouth.

On the Welsh Coast

Dawn arrives like a ghost
in this wilderness, as the mist settles here
and there near Llanelli
on the path down to the cove

in a thin valley of long grass.
A herd of wild ponies huddles together,
tans, browns, whites and spotted grays,
watching as I pass.

Above them on the hill a ruined castle,
its crenellated walls crumbling with age.
A stone falls while I wonder
at the lives of ancestors living here.

The waves lash cliffs below,
and the sky begins to lighten.
The birds have not begun to sing,
only the horses and I here at sunrise

with the spirits of defenders,
sentries on the ramparts
eyeing the sea for Viking ships,
marauders who would sack their home

leaving behind the dead
in the rubble of the dream of safety.
I remember the longbows,
the arrows and deadly vision,

strong hands and heavy grip, their
spirit unquenchable.
They breathe in me. I gather up
the light of morning and hold it in my arms.

The Weight of Air

Hoping for the ambulance to come,
waiting for someone to find me
in this ravine at the bottom of the road,

the car tipped on its side in the silence,
the windshield glass on the hood,
ice on salal, hail on the cedars,
the hemlocks.

Unable to move my left arm, unable to move.
A wrist subducted under a palm,
as the Pacific plate dives under the continent,
the pressure too great to hold,

unable to hold the weight of air
or tulips,
or stop the rivulet of blood
from sleeve to coat to shoes,

as the steering wheel smokes.
The car still in the form of a car,
my body still in the shape of a human,
a mind full of snow.

The side roads flashed by quickly,
as I slid away from steering, braking,
the car unwilling to change directions
at the curve, the grating rush, the crack of alders,
the jolt.

A stranger squats outside
the shattered window smiling at me.
Michael, coatless, dressed in T-shirt, jeans.
The cold is hard as a knife,
I am ready to change my life.

Blessing

May your life be woven as a Navaho blanket with threads of sky and earth.

May you dab your cloth with streaks of lightning, sea shells, crystals.

May your slippers be shod with cashmere and your pillow be satin smooth.

May California poppies line your path with a golden glow.

May the flanks of your hills be deep green, glazed with the yellow of mustard blooms.

And when you awaken in your blanket of light, may a little child take your hand.

INDEX

The poems of **Francine E. Walls** appear in *Writing Across Cultures: A Handbook on Writing Poetry and Lyrical Prose*, the anthology, *Peace Poets* v. 2 and numerous journals such as *Pontoon Poetry, Ekphrasis Journal, Passager Journal* and *By&By Poetry*. Born and raised in Seattle, Washington, she has also lived in Wales and Botswana. Francine received a doctorate in Education from Seattle University and worked in college and university libraries. Her blog at https://wordandimageworker.com pairs her poems with her photographs. A Pushcart Prize nominee, the poets who inspire her include Tomas Tranströmer, William Stafford, Jane Kenyon and Christine Valters Paintner.